DK READERS

Earth Smart

How to Take Care of the Environment

Written by Leslie G̲͟

DK

A Dorling Kindersley Book

"Hooray!" shouted Spencer.
"Here comes Aunt Charlotte
with some ice lollies!"
Aunt Charlotte was looking after
Spencer and his older sister, Sophie,
for the day.

Aunt Charlotte is a teacher.
Her classes are about the
environment – the world around us.
"We can all take good care
of the environment," she told
the children.

Aunt Charlotte gave
Sophie and Spencer
their ice lollies.
Spencer tore off
the wrapper
and tossed it
on the ground.
Sophie bent down to pick it up.
"We shouldn't drop litter," she said.
She put the wrapper into a nearby
rubbish bin.

Put a lid on it

Keep your environment clean
by putting litter in a rubbish
bin or taking it home. Keep
a lid on your bin at home
so rubbish doesn't blow away.

Aunt Charlotte agreed.
"We need to keep our planet clean
so it's a healthy place to live,"
she said.

Just then a rubbish lorry
stopped at the kerb.
A man emptied the rubbish bin
into the back of the lorry.

"Where is he taking
the rubbish?" asked Spencer.
"It goes to a landfill site," said
Aunt Charlotte.
"That's a huge pit in the ground
where rubbish is dumped, then
covered over with earth.
After a long time, the rubbish
breaks down and becomes soil."

Landfill site
Rubbish is spread
out and covered
with earth to keep
flies away and cut
down the smell.

"We should be careful about
the rubbish we throw out,"
said Aunt Charlotte.
"Some things are toxic."
"What's toxic?" asked Spencer.

"Things like cans of paint and batteries leak out dangerous chemicals that can get into our soil and water," replied Aunt Charlotte.

Leaking batteries

"If you have dangerous rubbish like this, get your parents to take it to a recycling centre, where it will be got rid of safely."

Batteries
You will throw away fewer batteries if you use rechargeable batteries or wind-up radios and torches.

Turning the handle charges the radio.

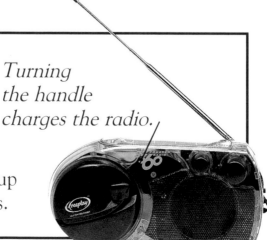

The children followed
Aunt Charlotte into the house.
"We throw away too much,"
Aunt Charlotte continued.
"We should recycle as
much as we can.

Drink cans
Aluminium cans
can be recycled over
and over again.
The metal always stays
strong and flexible.

That means saving things
like glass bottles,
plastic food wrappers
and cans, so they can be
reused or melted down
and turned into
something else."

*A vase made from
recycled glass*

"Let's set up recycling boxes,"
said Sophie.
She found three big boxes
and stuck labels on that said
"paper", "plastic", and
"glass and cans".

Spencer found some old
newspapers his mother
was going to throw away.
He put them in the "paper"
recycling box.

15

"Another way to help our planet
is to save electricity,"
said Aunt Charlotte.
"Power stations burn fuel
to make electricity," she said.
"Smoke from the burning fuel
makes the air dirty."
Spencer coughed.
"We breathe the pollution,"
he said.
"Without clean air, we can get
sick," said Sophie.
Aunt Charlotte nodded.
"And so can our planet," she said.

"The pollution in the air traps heat and makes the planet heat up," explained Aunt Charlotte. "This is called global warming. Ice is melting at both the North and South Poles.

Melting snow
Global warming is making snow melt on Africa's tallest mountain, Mount Kilimanjaro.

This means there will be more floods, and people and animals will lose their homes."

"If we use less electricity,
we will make less pollution,"
said Aunt Charlotte.
"Do you know how we can
use less at home?" she asked.
"We can turn lights off when
we don't need them," suggested
Spencer, as he turned a light off.

"We can read
books instead of
watching TV,"
added Sophie.
The TV was on,
so Sophie
turned it off.

Later they all set out for the park. "Phew," said Spencer, as they walked beside a busy road. "What's that smell?"

"That's exhaust from the car engines," said Aunt Charlotte. "It pollutes the air."

"If we walk, we'll cut down on pollution," Sophie said.

Aunt Charlotte nodded.

They arrived at the park and
found a place to have a picnic.
"I like the plants and trees in
the park," said Sophie.
"Trees protect us from
air pollution," said Aunt Charlotte.
"They give off oxygen, which
we can breathe.
Trees and other plants make

the air
healthier.
They also
provide homes
for many kinds
of animals."

They opened a bag of strawberries.
"These are from your uncle's farm,"
Aunt Charlotte said.
"He grows them organically.
That means he doesn't
use chemicals that
can harm the
environment."

Pricey produce

Growing crops using chemicals is easier than growing them organically, so organic food costs more.

"Is that why the strawberries taste so sweet?" asked Sophie.

"Probably," laughed her aunt. "He sells them at the local farmers' market. As he doesn't travel far, he doesn't make much pollution."

On the way home,
Aunt Charlotte and the children
stopped at the supermarket.
They had to buy food for dinner.

"Let's choose food that's grown nearby," said Aunt Charlotte. They checked the labels to find food grown in their own country or nearby countries. They found beans, potatoes and chicken, and yoghurt for dessert.

As they went home, Sophie said,
"Thanks for teaching us to take
care of the planet, Aunt Charlotte.
Now we can help cut down
on pollution."
"And recycle," her aunt added.
Spencer picked a chewing gum
wrapper off the ground.
"And I won't drop litter!" he said.

Save the environment

Remember the four Rs: **Reduce** the amount of things we use so that there's less to throw away, **reuse** things, **recycle** things to make new things, and **rethink** what we buy and use. These horse sculptures have been made from recycled materials.

Litter does not just make a place look unpleasant but also can be dangerous to animals and people. It can cause fires and is expensive to clean up.

Natural sources, such as the sun, wind and waves, can provide us with energy. They can produce heat and electricity without making pollution.

Trees provide us with better air quality, shelter us from the weather and attract birds and wildlife. By planting trees, we can have a healthier environment.